Cool Snowboarders

by Michael Sandler

Consultant: Christopher Del Sole
Snowboarding Expert
www.snowboarding.about.com

BEARPORT
PUBLISHING

New York, New York

Credits

Cover and Title Page, © Blend Images/Superstock; TOC, © Photostio/Shutterstock; 4, © Stefan Eisend/Imago/Icon SMI; 5, © Jeff Curtes/jeffcurtesphoto.com; 6, Courtesy of Tom Sims; 7, Courtesy of Brunswick Corporation; 8L, © Peter Grumann/The Image Bank/Getty Images; 8R, © Maureen Falk; 9, © Dan Carr/dancarrphotography.com; 10L, © moodboard/Corbis; 10R, © Marc Piscotty/Icon SMI; 11, © Stefan Eisend/Imago/Icon SMI; 12, © GEPA/Imago/Icon SMI; 13, © Andrew Meares/FairfaxMedia.com.au; 14, © Karl Weatherly/Corbis; 15, © Andrew Miller/Andrewmillerphotos.com; 16, © Doug Pensinger/Getty Images; 17, © AP Images/Lionel Cironneau; 18, © Andrew Miller/Andrewmillerphotos.com; 19, © AP Images/Nathan Bilow; 20, © Sveinung Svendsen; 21, © Marc Piscotty/Icon SMI; 22, © Alex T Roberts/alextroberts.com.

Publisher: Kenn Goin
Senior Editor: Lisa Wiseman
Creative Director: Spencer Brinker
Photo Researcher: Daniella Nilva

Helmets are a snowboarder's most important piece of safety gear. If you try snowboarding, wear one. It's the only way to snowboard.

Library of Congress Cataloging-in-Publication Data

Sandler, Michael, 1965-
  Cool snowboarders / by Michael Sandler.
     p. cm. — (X-moves)
  Includes bibliographical references and index.
  ISBN-13: 978-1-59716-949-3 (library binding)
  ISBN-10: 1-59716-949-8 (library binding)
  1. Snowboarding—Juvenile literature. I. Title.

 GV857.S57S26 2010
 796.939—dc22
                          2009005547

For more information, write to Bearport Publishing Company, Inc., 101 Fifth Avenue, Suite 6R, New York, New York 10003. Printed in the United States of America.

10 9 8 7 6 5 4 3 2 1

Contents

Cracking the Sky

Snowboarder Ingemar Backman flew up the huge curved wall of the **quarterpipe**. He reached the top, then soared above the **lip**. He rose into the sky—higher and higher.

At the top of his 25-foot (7.6-m) **backside air**, Ingemar reached down and grabbed his board. Then he swooped back down to the snowy ground like a graceful, diving bird. He landed his trick perfectly, arms thrown up in the air. No rider had ever flown so high before. One snowboarder said, "Ingemar was the first guy to crack the sky."

Swedish snowboarder
Ingemar Backman

4

Ingemar landing his record-breaking trick in Riksgränsen, Sweden, in 1996

In 1996, Ingemar's backside air set a record for highest **air** from a quarterpipe. It wasn't broken until 2001 when Heikki Sorsa flew even higher.

Building the Board

Snowboarding seems simple—just stand on a board and speed down a snowy hill. However, without the right board, that is pretty hard to do.

Unlike skis, which are centuries old, snowboards are a recent invention. In the 1930s, people tried standing on simple wooden sleds, but they were hard to control. Then, in 1965, Sherman Poppen joined two skis together and added a rope. Kids loved his "Snurfer," but it still wasn't snowboarding.

Finally, in the 1970s, Jake Burton found the secret to building a good snowboard. He added straps, or **bindings**, like those used on skis to keep riders' feet stuck to the boards. Now riders could fly!

Tom Sims created an early version of the snowboard in 1963.

Many early snowboard builders, such as Tom Sims and Dimitrije Milovich, were skateboarders or surfers who thought it would be fun to use their street and surf skills on the snow.

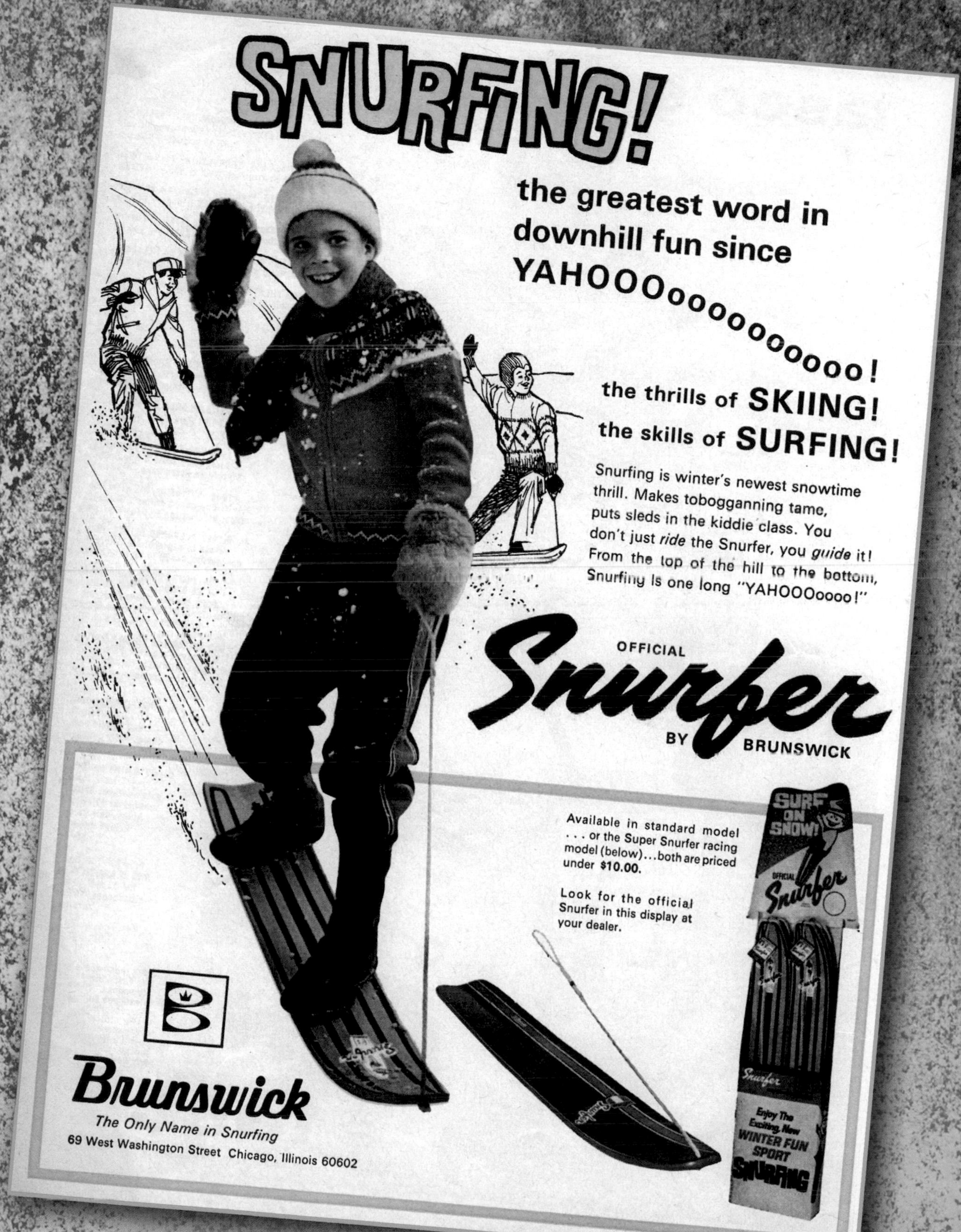

Snurfers weren't snowboards, but they were a lot of fun.

The Outlaw Sport

By the early 1980s, kids were trying snowboarding on the **ski slopes**. They weren't always welcome, however. Sometimes, snowboarders flew out of control as they barreled down the mountains and bumped into skiers.

Snowboarders also bothered skiers because they didn't follow all the rules. Just like skateboarders, they saw ordinary objects as places to do tricks. They jumped onto picnic tables. They did **rail grinds** down stairways. They **ollied** over benches.

Many ski resorts **banned** snowboarders, forcing them to find other places to ride. By the 1990s, however, snowboarders and skiers had learned to get along.

Skiers and snowboarders didn't always like to share the slopes.

NO SNOWBOARDING

This snowboarder uses picnic tables to perform a trick.

Early snowboard **promoter** Jake Burton traveled to ski resorts asking owners to allow snowboarding. He also trained snowboard users on how to safely mix with skiers and to obey resort rules.

Freestyle Snowboarding

There are several styles of snowboarding, but freestyle is the most popular. Freestyle riders do tricks similar to those done by skateboarders, but they **adapt** them for the slopes. Snowboard ramps are like those found in skate parks—quarterpipes and **halfpipes**. Instead of concrete, however, these pipes are made from snow.

Freestyle snowboarders enter the pipes and shoot up the walls. Sometimes they fly past the lip and do tricks in the air. Top boarders such as Danny Kass, Travis Rice, and Torstein Horgmo keep pushing the limits with even bolder moves.

A halfpipe

Danny Kass in midair

Freestyle legend Terje Haakonsen has a special trick named after him—the Haakon flip. To do it, he shoots into the air backward, flips, spins twice, and then lands going forward!

Race Snowboarding

Racing is another popular snowboarding style. Racers ride downhill and **carve** sharp turns along the way at incredible speeds. Sometimes they hit 70 miles per hour (113 kph). On zigzag **slalom** courses, racers move left-right-left around posts and panels called gates.

Snowboarders usually don't race in a group. Instead, they take turns. They ride down the same slope, one by one, trying to get the fastest time.

Only in **boardercross** races do snowboarders race together. They start as a group, racing in a pack to the finish. Along the way, they slip, slide, and slam through narrow turns and over steep jumps.

American Shaun Palmer (#13) is a legend in both slalom and boardercross.

Snowboard speed record holder Darren Powell

Australian Darren Powell is the world's fastest snowboarder. In 1999, Darren sped down a French slope at a blazing 125 miles per hour (201 kph). Ten years later, still no one had broken his record.

Freeriding

When riders were kept off the ski slopes during the early days of snowboarding, they often headed into the woods. Today, the wilderness is still the best place for another style of snowboarding—freeriding. Boarders who freeride skip the resorts and smooth, machine-**groomed** ski slopes. Instead, they head for the **backcountry** to find the wildest rides. Some places are so **remote** that snowboarders have to be dropped off by helicopter.

Freeriders don't leave out the tricks as they fly down the mountainsides. They just do them on cliffs, boulders, and glaciers instead of man-made ramps and halfpipes.

Backcountry snow sports can be dangerous. Craig Kelly, one of the greatest snowboarders ever, died in an **avalanche** during a ski trip in British Columbia, Canada.

Craig Kelly

Freerider Nick Russell jumps over a cliff.

Competitions

Competitions have been part of snowboarding since its earliest days. Today, snowboarders test their skills at the U.S. Open, the Winter **X Games**, Norway's Arctic Challenge, and even the Olympics.

Snowboarding became an Olympic sport in 1998. Today, medals are awarded in slalom, boardercross, and halfpipe competitions. In halfpipe events, judges score freestyle snowboarders on style, technique, and amplitude. Amplitude means how high the boarders can fly.

The X Games include an event called slopestyle where snowboarders perform tricks on a steep slope filled with boxes, rails, and jumps. They receive points for the style and difficulty of their tricks.

A great last run helped Jenny Jones win the 2009 Winter X Games gold for slopestyle.

Women and men compete in separate divisions at snowboarding competitions. At the 2006 Winter Olympics, in Turin, Italy, American Hannah Teter took gold in the women's halfpipe competition.

Top Tricks

Slopestyle and halfpipe competitions are always won by the boarders who can do the coolest tricks. These moves continue to get wilder and, sometimes, more dangerous. Like skateboard tricks, they often include spins. Snowboarders fly so high that they can do plenty of turns before they hit the ground.

While most skateboarders are happy with a 720—two full spins in the air—snowboarders go for more. Shaun White took **superpipe** gold at the 2008 Winter X Games with a stunning final run that included a 1260. That's three and a half turns in the air!

Young New Hampshire snowboarder Chas Guldemond is a master of the 1260. He's also one of the very first to land a 1440—four turns!

Shaun White flies through the air with his snowboard above the superpipe.

Shaun White, one of the world's best riders, has won gold medals at both the X Games and the Winter Olympics.

Even Higher

Snowboarding is still a new sport. Racers are constantly chasing speed records. Freeride snowboarders are always searching for wild new **terrain**. Freestyle riders such as Travis Rice and Terje Haakonsen keep striving for cooler tricks and higher airs.

Once, skiers didn't like snowboarders on their slopes. Now they just try to keep up. **Freeskiers** follow snowboarders into halfpipes, trying to do their tricks and copy their moves.

In 2008, one freeskier even broke a snowboarding record for highest air from a quarterpipe. The snowboarders didn't care. They knew they were the very first to "crack the sky."

Terje setting the new air record

On March 5, 2007, Terje made a record-breaking 32-foot (10-m) quarterpipe air. A year later, freeskier Simon Dumont did a 35-foot (11-m) air. Still, Terje holds the snowboarding-only record.

Travis Rice, shown here, performed one of 2008's best tricks, a switch backside double cork 1080. This complicated trick involves three full turns and two flips in the air.

Snowboarding 101

To snowboard down the biggest mountains or halfpipes, and perform the toughest tricks, snowboarders need special gear.

Helmet
Keeps your head safe if you fall

Goggles
Keep your eyes safe from wind, blowing snow, and the sun's blinding rays

Freestyle Board
Best ride for tricks

Nose
The front tip; turned up so you can glide across the snow without digging in

Sunblock
Put it on your face to protect yourself from the strong sun

Bindings
Keep your boots attached to the board

Jacket and Pants
Should be waterproof and windproof

Stomp Pad
A resting place for your back foot when it's out of the bindings

Gloves
Protect your hands from snow and cold

Waist
The narrow part of the board

Edges
A steel strip that goes around the entire board; it cuts into the snow to help you turn and stop

Tail
The back tip of the board

Boots
Should be comfortable and support your ankles

Glossary

adapt (uh-DAPT) to change to fit the environment or terrain

air (AIR) a trick in which a snowboarder rides into the air

avalanche (AV-uh-*lanch*) a large amount of snow, ice, or earth that suddenly moves down a mountain at a fast speed and without warning

backcountry (BAK-kuhn-tree) a remote, undeveloped area

backside air (BAK-side AIR) an air trick done with a snowboarder's back facing the object he or she is launching off of

banned (BAND) ordered to stay out; prohibited from using

bindings (BYNE-dingz) mechanical devices that attach boots to snowboards or skis

boardercross (BORD-ur-krawss) a snowboarding event in which racers start in a group on a narrow course; each trying to be the first across the finish line

carve (KARV) to make a turn cleanly without sliding or skidding

freeskiers (FREE-skee-urz) skiers who do extreme tricks or ski in wild, backcountry terrain

groomed (GROOMD) when snow is made smooth for easy skiing and snowboarding

halfpipes (HAF-pipes) U-shaped snow structures used for freestyle snowboarding tricks

lip (LIP) the upper edge of a halfpipe or quarterpipe

ollied (OL-eed) when a snowboarder is lifted off the ground by springing off the tail of the snowboard

promoter (pruh-MOH-tur) a person who tries to build the popularity of a sport or activity

quarterpipe (KWOR-tur-*pipe*) a curved wall made of snow that is one half of a halfpipe

rail grinds (RAYL GRINDEZ) tricks done by a snowboarder down the length of a handrail

remote (ri-MOHT) far away

ski slopes (SKEE SLOHPS) pathways on mountainsides that are specially prepared for skiers and snowboarders to ride down

slalom (SLAHL-uhm) a downhill event that includes quick turns around a set of obstacles called gates

superpipe (SOO-pur-*pipe*) a halfpipe with 18-foot-high (5-m) walls

terrain (tuh-RAYN) type of ground or land surface

X Games (EKS GAMZ) an extreme sports competition held every year

Bibliography

Brisick, Jamie. *Have Board Will Travel: The Definitive History of Surf, Skate, and Snow.* New York: HarperCollins (2004).

Daniells, Greg. *Let it Rip: The Ultimate Guide to Snowboarding.* Edison, NJ: Chartwell Books (1997).

Snowboarder magazine

Transworld Snowboarding magazine

Read More

Barr, Matt. *Snowboarding.* Pleasantville, NY: Gareth Stevens (2008).

Higgins, Matt. *The Insider's Guide to Action Sports.* New York: Scholastic (2006).

Kleh, Cindy. *Snowboarding Skills.* Buffalo, NY: Firefly (2002).

Schweitzer, Karen. *Shaun White.* Broomall, PA: Mason Crest (2009).

Learn More Online

To learn more about snowboarding's tricks, stars, and competitions, visit
www.bearportpublishing.com/X-Moves

Index